*   *   *

She DISRUPTS IT! You Can Too!

Bonnie

Thank you for your friendship and support

Annette

* * *

She DISRUPTS IT! You Can Too!

Four Powerful Strategies of Successful I.T. Women

Dr Annette Gibbs-Skervin

＊　＊　＊

Disclaimer

In order to maintain their anonymity, I have changed the names of the women interviewed and quoted in this book. The quotes were selected to reflect the combined experience of these women and are not meant to describe a particular person, event, company, or location.

In addition, throughout this book, fictional stories have been added to provide context for the strategies discussed. Names, characters, businesses, places, events, and incidents are either the products of the author's imagination or used in a fictitious manner. Any resemblance to actual persons, living or dead, or actual events is purely coincidental

* * *

Acknowledgments

I want to acknowledge and thank the women who contributed their time to this study. Their willingness to be interviewed and to share their stories is an expression of their success and their commitment to helping other women succeed.

It is my desire that this return on their investment will honor their voices.

Table of Contents

Preface

Andrea is TIRED. As she navigates up the road to her house, she considers driving by and just taking a moment to regroup before facing her family. Once again, she has put in a long day and worked late into the evening, after promising herself that this time she would leave early to work out. But once again, a 5 p.m. "crisis" landed on her lap. Not that she couldn't handle it — she knew when she took on this global role that this was going to be a challenge. And she loves a challenge. Once again she was told — "When you deliver this transformation, you will demonstrate to us that you're ready for that VP role." But that story is getting old. And today 5 Vice President promotion announcements were made — all for male colleagues. Funny how those colleagues seem to go home before her, have larger teams and less responsibility, and still get promoted!

"What am I doing wrong?" she wonders out loud. "Does this job really make sense for me anymore?" She's given up a lot: moved locations, sacrificed family time and some of her own personal goals. She has delivered results, turned around failing projects, and driven innovation. She is rated highly — and still the promotion eludes her. She has been sent to leadership training for women, minorities, and high-potentials. Still no promotion. One of the men who attended that training with her was actually one of those named in the promotion announcement. Great!

So, the questions come again. "What are my options?" "Should I leave?" "Will it be different in another company?" "But I've invested too much in this company to leave now — who would pay me the salary I'm getting?" "Do I really want to have to start this political game all over again?"

Are you Andrea? Do you long for the golden pathway that takes you off the constant merry-go-round of broken promises of promotions and unfulfilled potential? Do you want to be one of those women who have broken through the I.T. glass ceiling and made it into that club at the top? Do you want to create and live your success story?

You can begin by listening to the stories and wisdom of the women I interviewed for this book. They have achieved that professional breakthrough and know how to drive innovative disruption in I.T.! They are senior executives, CIOs, I.T. CEOs, Partners, and Vice Presidents. They work for companies of various sizes — for Fortune 500 companies, large companies, and mid-size companies. They work for a wide range of industries and for Information Technology (I.T.) and non-I.T. companies. Their backgrounds are different, but they are united by a drive to help other I.T. women succeed and overcome the roadblocks they face on their paths to the top. In fact — they're they ultimate disrupters...breaking through the expected, the status quo.

This book merges the experiences and advice of these women to help you create your own "DISRUPT IT!® Plan": your ultimate guide to success as a female I.T. leader. The following chapters, and the supporting resources at www.disruptitleader.com/SheDisruptsIT, will unlock the strategies that these women used and provide you with practical information to apply to your own career. They will move you from frustration and doubt to clarity, empowerment, and results.

So, are you ready to create your own DISRUPT IT!® Success Story?

Chapter 1

✳   ✳   ✳

The Women Who DISRUPT IT!®

In my search to learn how successful I.T. women made it to the top, I interviewed over 40 female I.T. leaders across the country and explored five aspects of their leadership journey:

* their definition of success,
* their training,
* their motivation for making I.T. a career,
* the barriers to their success, and
* the strategies and skills they employed to thrive in spite of these barriers

As you read about the journeys of these women, you may be surprised to see similarities to your own journey!

Defining Success

"If I'm not loving what I'm doing, then it isn't what I'm meant to be doing. If I don't feel successful, I won't be successful." (Lucy)

How do you define success? What does it mean for you personally? What does it mean to you on a professional level? The women I interviewed were clear on what success meant to them — and it was usually based on the expectations they set for themselves versus the expectations or standards of society. For them, success meant

* setting and meeting personal goals,
* happiness,
* making a difference in the lives of others,
* delivering results successfully,
* loving what you do, and
* receiving recognition through compensation.

Be aware that, like these women, your definition of success will influence your satisfaction with your personal and professional life. In Paige's words:

"When I leave this world, I want to be able to say there is something that I made that made this place a better place."

Her definition of success is making a difference in the world, and once she achieved that, then she would be content. Consider carefully what you truly feel would bring you satisfaction — how does your definition of success measure up to what you are doing today?

What Is The Proper Training to Be Successful In I.T.?

The answer may surprise you! Successful I.T. women come from both technical and non-technical educational backgrounds. Over 40% of the women I interviewed started with educational qualifications outside of I.T. or technology, with undergraduate degrees from fields as diverse as history, English literature, accounting, economics, business management, psychology, and mathematics. Other women were attracted to technology or the sciences during their educational journey. Some could distinctly remember being encouraged to embrace their ability and interest in mathematics and science. A few entered I.T. through programs that encourage an interest in technology

(STEM programs) in high school. These programs' results support the benefits of encouraging girls and women to embrace success in science, technology, mathematics, and engineering (STEM), feeding the pipeline of women coming up in this field.

Once they entered the I.T. field, these women were inspired to continue to train, learn, and grow in it because of their passion. They spoke about the ways technology drives business results and successful outcomes. They enjoyed the ability to collaborate with business partners, the challenge and excitement of being in an industry that was constantly changing and growing, and the wide range of career opportunities available. Erica told me that she values the uniqueness of

> *"the skills that I have that make it a lot easier to collaborate with businesses. I can explain to them how we got to the point where we are, what we need to do to move forward, where their gaps are, which a lot of technical people don't have the ability to convey in a way that can be well received."*

Motivation is as important as formal training. So, what is your motivation? What brought you into the I.T. field, and what makes you want to stay in it? What excites and gets you happy to go to work each day? What makes you want to learn more, do more, explore more in order to get to the top of this exciting field? We will continue to discuss motivation in other sections of this book and help guide you to a point where your motivation and success collide!

Barriers to Success

Of course, we can't have a discussion about successful women without also addressing some of the challenges that they faced along the way. Their answers won't surprise you!

* Experiencing a work environment that is "hostile" to women and minorities.
* Being excluded from the "old boys' club."
* Facing the backlash of ethnic or gender stereotyping, and
* Reporting to unsupportive bosses or supervisors.

Workplace Hostility

Experiencing a work environment that was "hostile" to women and minorities was overwhelmingly the top issue these women faced in their careers. Many could point to the transition of their environment from being openly sexist or racist to the current types of micro-inequities that can impact career progression, performance reviews, and assignment of key projects. Features of this type of environment include:

*   Tokenism — when you are the only woman or perhaps the only woman AND person of color in your department, location, leadership level, or subsidiary.

"In this particular environment, we have very few women of color in leadership roles. I am typically the only person of color at the table in a position of authority. It's challenging because I don't want to have the separation." (Lucy)

*   Lack of air cover — when you don't have a senior executive or leader who has your back or provides the extra support available to white male peers
*   Lack of political support — when you are not provided with the help, insights, sponsorship, or mentorship to successfully navigate the organizational culture. You are not privy to the politics that govern the organization and its culture.

"... I used to think that if you do a phenomenal job, they're going to come and give it to you. They don't, and that's a rude awakening .... I felt like I had to prove ten times more, I had to deliver ten times more than somebody who was playing these politics." (Paige)

Exclusion from the boys' club

There is also the explicit (and implicit) exclusion from the "old boys' club." Women find that it is impossible to be fully accepted into those networks — a woman may gain only partial acceptance or be invited to only certain activities. Charmaine states,

"Being included in one-off discussions, being consulted because people value your opinions. I think as a woman you're least likely to be in that inner circle."

Sound familiar? An interesting parallel to not feeling included in the old boys' club is that some women felt excluded when men did not feel comfortable acting like men around them. Could it be that in our politically correct society men are not comfortable bringing their natural personalities to the table? Ava spoke about her efforts to get into the boys' club by understanding sports, but also stated,

> "... yeah, it helps you. But in other cases, it doesn't. Because they still treat you like the 'Lady.' So they can't say the F* word in front of you, or they can't say the bad words or have the raunchy conversations in front of you...so as much as you try, you're still excluded."

You can't be technical...you're a woman!

Whether it was not being taken seriously, or being considered less capable as their male peers, these women have all experienced at some point in their careers the assumption that they are not technical or that they can't understand technology because of their ethnicity or gender. They also experienced a more generalized stereotyping: that as women, they are incapable of managing a high-level position. Vanessa discussed the impact of this stereotyping:

> "... the higher you want to go, that's when people say, "Oh, she's a woman. You think she can manage this much stress? And she has kids. She has four kids at home, do you think she can balance? How is she able to work effectively?"

These women were in situations where they were not expected to be technically capable or assertive. They spoke about the backlash and labels given to them when they spoke up, were not intimidated by others, provided their opinion, pushed back, were direct, or were just vocal. While these behaviors were expected and even celebrated in their male colleagues, in the women's case, they were labeled bossy, bitchy, aggressive, emotional, or combative. However, Nicole felt that the backlash was restricted to her male counterparts in I.T. and that her business partners were more receptive to her style:

> "I almost feel like sometimes the I.T. executives perhaps don't know what to do with me, because I am as assertive and as challenging as they are, and they're almost not expecting it from a woman."

Black women still bear the additional burden of being labeled as an "angry black woman" when they are assertive. As Samantha stated,

> *"I think that if you're reasonably intelligent, or let's say you're extremely intelligent and you're a black woman, and you don't tolerate bull — you're scary".*

Some of those I interviewed believed in adopting a more masculine style in order to succeed in the male-dominated arena of I.T. However, they received an additional backlash from men, who were expecting a more "feminine" approach. Bottom line — there is no safe ground for women if your goal is to satisfy assumptions based on gender-based stereotypes!

Unsupportive bosses or supervisors

One woman described this barrier succinctly:

> *"The most difficult challenges in my career have been working for someone that doesn't appreciate the work you do, and doesn't value what you do, and pretty much doesn't even give you the time and space to even find out who you are." (Lucy)*

This is how the unsupportive bosses or supervisors behaved:

* They showed their discomfort with spending time with women.

> *"... they spend time with people that they're most comfortable with. And they're not comfortable spending time with me." (Samantha)*

* They questioned the credibility of the women who work for them and/or didn't value their skills and styles.

> *"My credibility is on the line at all times, as a woman .... I had that one manager who I started reporting to, and he kept looking at the other guy like, 'Is*

what she saying right?' I had to get him to that point where he wasn't turning his head anymore." (Jade)

* They did not award women with the career opportunities needed for visibility or promotion.

"The hardest part ... whether it's making Partner, whether it's making VP... [is the] perception people have of [you].... The only way that this question can be answered is through relationships and visibility. These [promotion] decisions are based on people knowing you." (Sarah)

* They did not provide women with the clear feedback that they needed to improve, avoid political missteps, and be positioned for success within the company.

"I had never gotten that type of feedback from any manager before — and I have asked. Especially men. You try and get men to give you feedback, and it's like pulling teeth." (Lucy)

How I.T. Women Not Only Survive but *Thrive* in the Face of Adversity

Despite these barriers to success, these women did not let their circumstances define them. They all developed specific strategies for success, which were remarkably consistent across the group, while leveraging their personality traits and leadership styles.

The role of personality and outlook on life

So, is there a specific personality type that contributes to being successful? The top personality traits that I identified in these successful women were

* Dependability, loyalty, wisdom, and forthrightness,
* Drive, determination, and confidence,
* A sense of fun and optimism,
* Being caring, compassionate, and willing to help others.

They describe themselves as Type A personalities: overachievers, hardworking, no-nonsense, and results focused. Or as Charmaine explains,

> "I think people tend to describe me as a very focused, no-nonsense, get-it-done person."

Their friends know that they are dependable and can be counted on.

> "I think people see me more as a problem solver and a go-to person to help them clean things up." (Erica)

They are optimistically pragmatic, always seeing the best in the situation but not shying away from facing and stating the unvarnished truth. These women have a strong internal compass — integrity and honesty are values they embody and that they expect from their team.

They are also self-confident and have a strong sense of self-worth. Their take-charge character, while positive, can also be seen as controlling (as mentioned in the stereotyping section). Paige described herself in this way:

> "Once I set my mind to it, I get focused and get it done. I would say that's pretty much my style, whether it's here or it's at home."

It follows that they are not intimidated by a person's level or expertise. They will challenge those in authority, a style that may make others (especially Caucasian men) uncomfortable. Alexis said that she would be described as

> "fearless. I'm not afraid to challenge management."

The women described their personalities as caring and compassionate with a desire to help, empower, and support others. Hannah describes herself as someone *"that has very strong, deep listening skills and that always looks at empowering and helping people."*

They are loyal and supportive of their friends and family, to those that they have let into their circle.

"I'm a rough, tough cream-puff. I do have a soft side, but I tend to project a much tougher exterior." (Charlotte)

In-spite of having a driven and focused personality, of being Type A, many of the women also described themselves as fun-loving. This is another trait that they bring to their leadership style, and many prioritized this aspect as an important factor in the teams that they lead. This trait also helps them manage the stress that they face in their challenging roles. They have the ability to laugh at their situation, to have fun with friends, and to decompress.

They women I interviewed tend to be optimistic in their approach to life in general and to particular situations, having a *glass half full* mentality. This is a coping strategy that also helps them navigate difficult situations.

"My close friends would say that I'm funny, that I laugh about everything, which is true. Generally, when we talk, because some of the situations can be difficult that we face, and because we're each other's support system, we tend to look at things with humor." (Alexis)

So as you can see, your perspective on life is critical to your success! Let's take a more careful look at the common aspects of the successful woman's personality and at the three ultimate drivers of her success (and yours!). Successful I.T. women use

* confidence,
* determination, and
* willingness to both give *and* receive support from family and friends.

Over 50% of the women I spoke to emphasized the importance of self-confidence. They express confidence in the skills they bring to the table, the value of those skills in their current environment, and their confidence in how marketable those skills are outside their current workplace.

> *"That was my motto — don't quit. But if I do, I can get a job. So it was also that belief in myself that I've always been very marketable." (Emma)*

As confident leaders, these women have learned not to let others intimidate them or abuse them. In fact, they refuse to be intimidated or abused by others. This extends to being confident when leading team members with higher education levels, varying backgrounds, and different levels of expertise. As Hannah states,

> *"I have found that it's the person that makes the professional, nothing else...so I just don't get intimidated easily, and I just move on."*

The women's confidence is innate but also comes from investing in their skills, keeping up-to-date in their area of expertise, and ensuring that they continue to develop the knowledge and experiences to be successful in their current role or environment. *So dust off that development plan and prioritize it!*

What is remarkable about the women I spoke with is not only their high levels of confidence but also their almost single-minded determination to succeed and to achieve every goal they set for themselves. Samantha described it:

> *"...part of the reason that I've been able to persevere is that I've never given myself the option of not doing it."*

"I do not quit" or "I persevere" is what most of the women told me. Erica described her personality in this way:

> *"...it's kind of that of a pit bull. I find something and then I dig into it and I just fight and fight and fight and fight, until I get what I want."*

In line with this attitude, they do not give themselves any options for failure, nor do they make excuses (e.g., based on ethnicity or gender):

> "I can play a lot of cards — I can play the race card; I can play the gender card. But to me, those are all excuses. My goal, and the bigger reward for me, is that I thrive in spite of all the negative stuff that's happening." (Ava)

The women I spoke to also express their determination as an ability to be *thick skinned* and their deliberate decision to turn a blind eye to prejudice.

> "...knowing that you're not always going to be treated fairly in every situation and being cognizant of that, but not letting that stop you or derail you is crucial. I think you have to put it in perspective and move on to something better." (Charmaine)

All acknowledge that in their determination to succeed, they need to be assertive and will adopt that behavior even if it means that they will be labeled in a derogatory manner. In the words of Hannah,

> "I still believe that the cliché of 'I have to be a bitch to succeed' is true, especially in the world of I.T."

Their view of barriers was that none of them were unsurmountable. As Charlotte put it:

> "You look at it as, 'With these barriers and obstacles, how can I get around them?' I think you need that mindset — thinking of them as just like slight bumps in the road, as opposed to the complete roadblock that you can go no further."

Another key theme among these strong, independent women? They reach out to others! They welcome and nurture a support structure of friends and family that help to keep them on track. This personal network includes the people *on their side*, who are available to talk through issues, combat the negativity in the workplace, and provide the coping mechanisms needed to survive. Anna describes her personal support network in this way:

> "[W]hen you have good people around you — outside of the workplace — it really helps you deal with the negativity of the workplace, because you're not just defined by that job."

Remember that you must deliberately cultivate and nurture your personal network or support structure. It is interesting that in addition to devoting time to their professional success, these women took the time to build personal relationships that mattered. *I challenge you to take a moment and write down the names of those who you would consider part of your personal support group or network.* If your list is empty or short — don't panic. Consider this your wake-up call! The goal is not to have a long list — it is to have relationships that personally matter to you and to your core well-being. Take steps to build the relationships with those who are (or who you want to be) in your network.

Conclusion

You now understand the factors the I.T. female leader uses to define success and the common traits of her personality. You also have insights into how she thinks, what motivates her, and what barriers she faces and overcomes. She is confident and determined and has a strong support network. Many of you can see yourself reflected in the experiences, backgrounds, personalities, and motivations of these women; and many of you have faced similar barriers. These women are much like you!

Now let's take a closer look at exactly how she SUCCEEDS and how you can too!

Chapter 2

* * *

"It's Not Me, It's You!": How To Overcome Bias

* * *

Andrea had an overwhelming feeling of frustration as she walked out of a leadership meeting. Everyone at the table was trying to get their point across and defending their budget and project choice. When Raymond, the VP for I.T. Sales & Marketing, opened the floor for recommendations to close the $500,000 budget gap, Andrea was ready to propose the vendor strategy that could streamline their procurement and provide opportunities to negotiate better contracts. It was an idea that she had floated with a few of her peers, and she knew it could get traction.

As she started to explain the idea, Bill, Director of ERP systems, spoke up and shot it down, stating that it would be too risky for his area if his primary vendor was not allowed to continue their work with him. Bill then went on to "remind" Raymond of the importance of his ERP project. Andrea had seen this move before — the power play that Bill used whenever he disagreed with an idea, usually her idea. Then the others around the table quickly followed his lead — including Raymond. In addition to its benefit to the company, her cost savings objective was a key deliverable for her goals this year. Without it, her team's production and personal ratings were at risk. As Andrea watched the dynamics from the team unfold, she noticed that she was the most vocal of the few women on the team, but the other women were from HR and Finance. What could she do to shift this power play?

* * *

What Do Successful I.T. Women Tell Us about Overcoming Bias?

"Wow — I can't believe that just happened." Yes — your point was just ignored and then repeated by a man and suddenly "heard." Or you got that shocked look when your colleague, who you were working with remotely, met you for the first time and realized that you're not *white*. Or you just came out of a meeting where it seemed that the men "forgot" there was a woman in the room as they spoke about their clubbing the night before. Or maybe you work in an environment where your boss seems to spend more time with your male peers but is very uncomfortable in your presence. Maybe your male peer let it "slip" that you were hired only because they needed to fill the diversity quotient. What do you do?

The women I interviewed provided many stories of times they experienced implicit or explicit bias in their career. Although those negative experiences occurred at various stages of their careers, they refused to be restricted by someone else's perception of their gender or ethnicity. They advise other women to ignore the limitations based on the stereotypical assumptions of others and instead to focus on their own ability.

"It's how you react or don't react to these things that's going to make the difference. Sometimes people are just ignorant, and that's just the way it is. You've got to know that, and get some thick skin, and just keep going where you have to go." (Lucy)

In light of the additional opposition that women and ethnic minorities experience, women need to be above average — setting high personal objectives and goals, and committed to perform and deliver with excellence. In the words of Mia:

> "And so the message for me to women is, you have to work harder to get to the goal, more than other people. You have to be really, really good at what you do. You have to be better than others. You have to be above average."

What do you want them to see when they look at you?

These successful women also spoke about professionalism, image, and managing one's sexuality. In contrast to the discussion of valuing one's unique strengths, these women warn that flamboyancy and strong ethnic cues can distract their peers and clients from focusing on their ability. They offered several examples of situations where client-facing or leadership presentation opportunities were denied based on an employee's choice of hairstyle, clothing, body art, and other personal style choices. Charlotte states:

> "[Y]ou also have to be able to present yourself in a way that is not distracting from what you are trying to do. Sometimes you do have to be that vanilla version of yourself. By vanilla, I mean plain."

Although men may have the opportunity to be less formal, this is usually not an option for women. The burden is on women to always maintain a corporate, professional image. This advice is indicative of the *tightrope* or *balancing act* that women need to constantly maintain.

> "I would tell them that you have to be very careful about how you're being perceived in an organization. And oftentimes, because it is perception, it can be wrong. One of the pieces of advice that I would give is always make sure you're perceived in the highest light ... sometimes the way you dress and carry yourself can be perceived in a negative fashion." (Alexis)

So is it wrong to dress in a feminine manner? Not at all! But beware of the slippery slope of using flirting, provocative dressing, and other feminine cues in the workplace. They may help you at first...and then backfire.

> *"You've got to keep a good balance of being feminine and being comfortable in your own skin and being able to work with men and being extremely professional." (Lauren)*

The question you have to ask yourself is — what is the image that you want to project? What is your endgame? Do you want to be respected or liked? Do you want to have a date or a business partner? Dressing provocatively and behaving flirtatiously in the workplace is a power that women can wield against men who work for or with them. Be aware that sexual harassment is not just a male thing — it can go both ways.

The women I interviewed were clear about the need for women to manage their image, to remain professional at all times, and to be aware of inadvertent flirtatious actions. Some behaviors unconsciously play into the stereotypical roles of Mother, Daughter, or Sister. For example — are you always the one bringing cookies or treats for coworkers (i.e., playing the nurturing role)? Are you playing the role of going to your (older) male boss asking for advice and guidance (the daughter role)? None of these behaviors is bad in itself — just examine whether the behaviors are influencing how you are perceived as a professional in your organization or team.

The women I interviewed also spoke about their concern with women who appear to go in the opposite direction and who try to be like "one of the boys" in terms of dress and attitude. Bottom-line — be true to yourself and to your style while being aware of the perceptions that it may generate. Ask a trusted advisor at work to critique you. Or follow the example of some of my panel members who sought help from a professional image consultant. We all fall into the trap unconscious actions that may have served us well in past roles but may not be appropriate for the role we want to be promoted to.

Do they know you...the real you?

In addition to acting and looking the part of a successful I.T. professional, there is another key way to overcome bias: build relationships. It is only through getting to know
you that people can abandon any stereotypes that they may hold about you. Consider
Tanya's story:

* * *

*Sitting in Raymond's office for her performance review, Tanya went over the
feedback from her peers and business partners. One consistent comment
jumped off the page: "she seems reserved and aloof." She was surprised at
this — after all, she wasn't at work to make friends. She worked hard, getting in early, staying late, and even working from home some evenings. She
delivered results — as shown by her project performance. Yes, she didn't
go to the mixers after work, but who has time for that? And she wasn't one
for idle small talk — particularly when she didn't feel comfortable letting
people know about her personal life. She knew of men who seemed to share
everything that was happening about the latest sports game, about wives
and kids. She did not have children to talk about — and wouldn't talk about
them if she did. "Can't we just keep personal stuff out of work and focus on
the job?" she wondered*

* * *

Interestingly, many women are like Tanya. They separate their "work" persona from
their "home" persona and view the workplace as an environment where they need to
be guarded and careful. They view the workplace as an inappropriate environment to
build relationships — and earlier on their careers as individual contributors, this isolat-
ing behavior and results-only focus worked for them. However, to move to the level
of leadership, you need to develop effective relationships. Successful I.T. women overwhelmingly spoke about the need to build relationships and network, not just with
other women or people of color, but across the organization — irrespective of gender

and/or ethnic similarities. They emphasized the importance of building relationships with your supervisor, your peers, your business partners, and those at lower levels in the organization. They recommend deliberately working to increase the comfort level of all of those around you. Amber states:

> "You got to work up. You got to work sideways. You got to invest in those that are below you....Get your supervisor and your peers invested in your success. Because when you do that, they'll speak you up."

While purposeful relationships can provide the environment for exposure and can combat assumptions based on ignorance, they also require a willingness to go beyond the superficial conversation and to share more of yourself. Many times it will be up to you to build that bridge to the client, peer, boss, or team member. Learning about their interests and being able to interact with them will help you take the first steps across that bridge and encourage them to do the same with you. Effective networking requires the ability to be vulnerable and to trust. If you don't open up yourself, you cannot be authentic, and if you are not authentic, you can't build relationships. While your tendency may be to protect your private life and keep it private, understand that people relate to a person and experiences, not to a job or title. You need to find the personal connection with the person you are networking with. And in order to do that, you need to open up and take off the "boxing gloves" that you may be using to protect yourself from being exposed. For example, you may need to be prepared to share that story about the crazy moment you had with your daughter when she was young. Or the time you decided to fly to Paris on a whim. Or the challenges of getting over your fear of speaking publicly.

Of course there is the opposite extreme of sharing too much information. So, to those women who find themselves sharing a lot of their personal life at work, I would say — keep some of your private life private! Don't talk to your peers, boss, and team members about your personal life as if they were your friends. Let your network of friends and confidantes be the sounding board for truly personal information. Be deliberate and strategic about what you will share. You don't want a personal confidence to be discussed in a meeting that you're not in. For example, you don't want your plan to have another child becoming the topic of discussion in a succession planning meeting!

There is a balance between sharing no information (and therefore risking that people will fill in the gaps with whatever information they perceive to be true) and sharing too much information (which will only hurt you in the end and impact your professional image). If you are starting from either extreme, experiment by changing the way you start a relationship with a new mentor or co-worker. As with any relationship, you cannot predict what the response to shared information will be — and sometimes it may be negative or even stereotypical. The rules of relationship building in general apply to the workplace — it takes time to build trust.

Change your lens

When it comes to bias, realize that the problem is not yours — it's theirs. That is, you cannot control how someone responds to you based on their internal assumptions. But you do control your response to their behavior.

> "I don't think there were any issues with me believing that a woman can lead. I think there were other people's issues, in believing that a woman can lead .... So often you're dealing with other people's insecurities. and you're always dealing with other people's points of view, even when you're not dealing with it." (Anna)

As many of you know, facing blatant and subtle discrimination or opposition based on your gender and/or ethnicity is not a one-time event. This will continue to happen throughout your career. The bigger question is — what do you want to do about it? It's important that you come up with a game plan for how you will respond to the inevitable.

Now, I know that some of you are thinking: "That doesn't happen to me.... I'm tired of hearing of women or ethnic minorities complaining about being treated differently." Bear in mind that you have just uncovered the first step to working through this situation — that is, to adjust your lens. *Think about it.* Have you noticed that when you decide to change your car and start looking at a particular make and model, you suddenly start seeing those cars on the road? Were they always there? Yes. *What changed? Your focus! When the make and model of the car became important to you, you started to notice the cars that were already there.*

You will always find what you are looking for. If you believe that you will be treated differently because of your gender or ethnicity, then you risk interpreting all such situations through that lens. What does our team of experts recommend?

"Don't think of yourself as a woman in leadership. Just think of yourself as a person in leadership.... If you can think that way, then that's what you'll project. If you project that, other people will see it the same way." (Charlotte)

Change your lens. Instead of expecting that you will be treated differently because of your gender or ethnicity, focus on your ability. Do you define yourself as a woman in I.T. or as an I.T. leader? The answer to that question can make a difference in how you interpret situations *and* in how you are perceived. Whatever you believe becomes your truth, so define yourself in terms of strengths and ambitions, not in terms of ethnicity and/or gender.

Adapt to the "new country"

You are in a male-dominated field. I know — that's stating the obvious! But think of what would happen if you were working in a different country where people didn't speak your language. While they may be polite to you, when they get together, they will relax, speak in their own language, and exhibit their cultural norms. As an outsider, you may not understand either the language or the actions. For the insiders (the natives of the country), it will be business as usual, and they may even forget that there's an outsider in the room. What are your options? You can try to understand the language and culture of your new country, or you can remain the outsider.

Census data supports the fact that, as a woman in I.T., your "new country" is predominantly male. One way to learn the language or culture of your new country is to enable the assistance of "local guides" — mentors and sponsors. They can help you understand what works in your company and what does not! I learned this lesson the hard way when I started working at a new company early in my career. In my old company, an assertive, challenging style was applauded. However, unbeknownst to me at the time, my new company had a relationship-based culture that avoided confrontation or challenging discussions during meetings. So, when I used the challenging, confrontational style that my old company accepted at my first few meetings in my new company, I was accused of being combative and not being a team player! I quickly learned my lesson, and with the help of mentors, I worked to build relationships, learned how to challenge ideas in a way that would be heard in my new company, and adjusted my communication style.

Another tactic is to develop a thick skin and be less sensitive to the situations that you will face. Just like when you're in a foreign country, realize that the norms of the organizational culture that you're in are just that — norms. The "offender" may not realize that what he is saying is upsetting to you — or even intend to offend you.

"When you're entering a male-dominated field, you can't really be that sensitive person that you probably are at home." (Sophia)

Yes, there are situations that warrant a discussion with Human Resources — and this is not to recommend in any way that hostile work environments, sexual harassment, or discriminatory behavior be overlooked or accepted. However, as women working in a male-dominated environment, we need to be aware of the culture that we are in and make our own determination about where we set the bar. Successful I.T. women will tell you it is not worth your energy to respond to ignorance!

"Sometimes people are just ignorant, and that's just the way it is. You've got to know that, and get some thick skin, and just keep going where you have to go …. I don't waste my energy on people like that." (Lucy)

Build (and Maintain) a Reputation for Delivering with Excellence and Integrity

"You need to prove yourself. Whether it be to another man or to another woman….You need to show them what your capabilities are and what you can do beyond talk." (Olivia)

All the women interviewed spoke about the importance of performance, delivering the projects, services, initiatives, or performance objectives. They emphasized that for women and for women of color, the bar is set higher — and as a result, their results always need to be above average. Is this unfair? Probably. However, for many of you, whether you realize it or not — this is the reality of your environment. You will need to get used to the fact that (for the most part) you will work harder than your male counterparts. You will need to get used to the fact that you have to prove yourself — not just once, but continually. The solution? Establish a reputation for getting things done, delivering results, *and doing what you said you would do.* Credibility is built on performance and consistent delivery. To be viewed as a valued asset to the team, to be considered for opportunities for sponsorship, to be considered for the key projects and assignments, *you must deliver.*

This expectation of superior performance and integrity also extends to members of your team. Successful I.T. women know that the bar has been set high for them to succeed, and as a result they set high expectations for their team.

> *"My leadership style has been very much 'keep your word,' very much 'get shit done.'" (Mia).*

They recommend being very clear in communicating expectations and not tolerating underperformers:

> *"I have gotten this feedback that people that are high performers, they love working for me because they know what to expect. But people that are probably not high performers, that want to coast, they struggle." (Amber)*

It is important to never compromise your integrity. The commitment to a strong internal compass is a hallmark of these successful women. This is also an expectation of their team members.

> *"Integrity. I like people that are truthful. I like honesty. I like people that have a great work ethic. I like people that are respectful of others. I like people that like to have fun and smile and have joy in what they do at work. But I particularly*

like people with integrity. I had a difficult time working with people that lack integrity." (Anna)

Demonstrate Grace under Fire

* * *

It was a leadership meeting with the technology team reviewing the strategy for the next two years. Pauline, responsible for Strategy Planning, looked around the room at the attendees, who were all joking about the discussion at the bar they went to last night. She was used to it — as one of the few women in her department, and the only female leader on the team, she was usually excluded from those invitations. "Not that I would want to go and spend more time with them," she thought to herself. "I never enjoy having to try and fit into those events anyway! But it would have been nice to be asked." Peter. Of VP Enterprise Infrastructure, opened up the meeting, setting the stage for the presentation that Ralph, Director of Technology Transformation, was about to make. Pauline was new to the team, having transferred in from the I.T. Business Relationship team. She was still trying to get on Peter's schedule for regular 1–1s, but they had a good initial meeting, she thought.

Peter began. "Ralph's team has been working on the technology strategy for the next five years. I'm really excited about the direction that we are going to take our organization and the way we're going to deliver against our innovation goals." Turning to Pauline, Peter said, "Pauline — glad you are here! I know that this is going to be a very technical conversation, but I hope that you'll be able to follow as we go through this. Let's see if you'll understand enough of what's said so that you can develop a version of this presentation that even my wife would understand!" Peter laughed and so did the rest of the team. Pauline was stunned and for a moment at a loss for words. She knew that Peter had seen her background — and they had discussed her work history, which included her starting out as a network engineer, followed by several leadership positions in infrastructure. However, this was not the first time that Peter had made these types of statements that assumed she was just the "non-technical" woman in the room.

Not smiling, Pauline took a deep breath and looked directly at Peter. "Well Peter, given my technical background and experience, I am sure that I can pull together the type of presentation that we can use to sell this future strategy to our business partners." Inside, she was seething, but she carefully maintained her composure for the rest of the meeting.

* * *

Remember that as a leader and a woman, you are being watched ***all the time*** — even when you are being treated "unfairly." Were you passed over for that promotion? Were you given the responsibility of the next level but not given the stripes to support it? How you react in these times is critical. Are you a whiner, complaining to all who will hear you? Are you going to shut down because a situation is "unfair"? Are you going to let your ego get the better of you because the person you report to is not someone you respect? Take the time to get out of your own way and come up with a strategy for how you will deal with unfair situations and what you will do. That could include making a decision to stay or a decision to move to another role or company. The women I interviewed recommend that you check your ego (and hurt feelings) at the door, be professional at all times, and continue to manage to deliver against your objectives with excellence (and the right attitude!).

These women emphasized the importance of managing your emotions. This does not mean being emotionless. The work environment is not the place to respond emotionally *off the cuff* (this includes anger, crying, and other situation-inappropriate emotional responses). Of course, you can use anger to manage the situation — if that's the tool that you've selected to use and you are in control.

"It's not that you're going to tolerate anything that is negative towards you, you're going to feel it. It's how you handle it. It's how you react or don't react to these things that's going to make the difference." (Lucy)

The bottom line is to keep control of your emotions — your emotional response should be deliberate and intentional. This also extends to using humor to diffuse a situation. Plan ahead by thinking through some potential scenarios that you've faced or seen others face in the past. Spend a few moments describing the potential situation; then determine how you prefer to handle the situation. Then *practice, practice, practice!* Is the situation the inability to contain your anger when someone disparages your country of origin? Determine what your response should be, find a trusted partner (friend, co-worker, family member, etc.) who can role-play with you, and practice what you will say. Is the situation that you become defensive when your project results are being criticized or when you receive negative feedback? Determine how you will respond to criticism and negative feedback — and role-play some situations with your trusted partner. Remember to practice your verbal and non-verbal responses. Give your trusted partner enough information on the personalities that you will be interacting with so they can get into character. Why practice? Because preparation gives you control and feedback from someone you trust. Practice provides you with the confidence to respond in a manner that you can control.

Conclusion

As a leader, you will always face challenges. By ensuring that your focus is on outcomes, performance, the image that you project, and your adaptability to the I.T. culture, you can follow in the footsteps of the successful I.T. women who were interviewed. It is clear that success starts from within you, and the following chapter discusses how you can build the internal confidence you need as a leader.

Chapter 3

✳ ✳ ✳

Find and Use Your Confident Leader "Superpowers"

* * *

It was another shouting match — but that's just how Tony liked to run his meetings. You just never knew who would be the target that day. So everyone came to the meetings getting ready to defend their turf and attack if needed. As he started to talk about the latest system outage, Tony began to criticize the leadership team. Accusations flew as everyone started blaming others for the issue.

Tanya was ready — she knew this move from Tony, and they had spoken about it several times. She quickly reminded those in the meeting about the Enterprise Release Deployment report the leadership team had discussed last week. It was part of the new Deployment Process she implemented in order to manage the impact of project releases in the environment. At that time, she had highlighted the capacity risk, given the expected demand from the new Marketing Campaign. However, the recommendation was overridden with assurances from the Application VP that their releases would have a "manageable" impact on capacity.

Tanya carefully diffused the tension in the room by using her collaboration skills and pulling in some of the ideas that had surfaced in her earlier 1–1s with the team members. She ended the conversation with "So, now that we have some ideas on the table, let's discuss some actions we can take to solve this. I am also willing to head up a team to do a root-cause analysis of this issue and see what we can do to reduce the risk of this happening in the future."

* * *

What Successful I.T. Women Tell Us about Confident Leadership

What is confident leadership? Successful I.T., women like Tanya in our story above, are ready to face issues and challenges and to speak up! The women I interviewed knew their strengths or, as one woman called it, their "Superpower." They recommend having an unshakeable self-confidence, even if others don't share it, and emphasize the importance of aspiring women to be courageous and fearless.

> *"Be fearless, do not be afraid to speak up. I think sometimes, as women, we tend to hold back, whereas men feel more comfortable expressing themselves, good or bad." (Alexis)*

Anna builds on this point by discussing the confidence that women can gain from their skills and expertise:

> *"[I]t's also your confidence in how you look at yourself and your ability to trust what you're saying. And then trust that you deserve to be heard…. To be a leader, you have to have people willing to follow you. And as you see more and more people willing to follow you, you hone those skills."*

These successful I.T. women overwhelmingly confirmed that confidence comes from knowing your unique value and continuing to invest in yourself. It's reinforced by keeping your core values and integrity:

> *"I would say know yourself, know what you're comfortable with, know your style, deal with people in a way that you would want to be dealt with, be able*

to assess situations, and figure out how best you can operate in that environment. If there are ever cases where you feel that you can't operate as yourself, that you can't be true to yourself and feel good about yourself in what you're doing, then you need to find a different place to do what you do." (Charmaine)

Authenticity and integrity build trust. Think about it — why do used car salespeople have such a bad reputation? Because of the perception that they are not trustworthy. People build relationships with those whom they trust. The women I interviewed cited trust and integrity as one of the personal character traits or values that they expect from the members of their team. Being trustworthy extends to being reliable — doing what you said you would do. Women have the ability to build trust through authentic relationships and empathy.

There are two ends of the pendulum of authenticity and adaption. One extreme is rigid and insists that others accept a woman for who she is. The other extreme tries to change to please everyone. Neither approach provides long-term leadership success. So, instead of focusing on how others perceive you, focus on what you want to accomplish. Have a vision and a plan that drives your goals and directs what you need to accomplish during the current project, role, or interaction. Focusing on results and expected outcomes helps you put minor distractions, micro-inequities, and other potential barriers in perspective. It also helps you regain control of the situation — versus waiting for others to fight or step up on your behalf or giving into a victim mentality.

Building a Confident YOU

"You've got to be genuine, confident, and passionate about what you are doing." (Alyssa)

Confidence and courage: two simple words that are the foundation of success for women. It takes confidence to step up and lead. It takes confidence to bounce back after disappointment and loss — of a job, a promotion, a coveted role. Yet all of the women on the expert panel looked fear in the eye and won! How? Their success started with an inner confidence based on the knowledge of their strengths. Confidence and courage start with you knowing, using, and believing in your strengths.

"...the things that I've found that I could tap on that would make me separate from the rest of the members. I really tried to lean on those strengths." (Anna)

Your personal leadership brand

"[K]now what you are phenomenal in ... the one, two, or three things that are your superpowers, that you are absolutely happy doing, confident in, that nobody does like you. You don't think it's special because it doesn't require any effort from you. That's exactly the thing that makes you special." (Jessica)

Think about your strengths in terms of building your personal leadership brand. Consider the brands you know today. Whether it's a sporting good, a baby product, an investment service, or a theme park — if someone provides you with the name of the brand, a visual image comes to mind. You can visualize the product, and you know what it does. You can differentiate it from other similar products. You also know what it does not stand for. One airline may be known for its exclusive service and special amenities. Another airline may be known for its low-cost fares. Both are airlines — the brand message is the differentiator.

Building your personal brand is similar: you want people to know those things that define you! When they think of you, what comes to mind? Can they describe you in terms of your value and strengths? As a leader, if you don't define your personal brand, others will shape it for you. And as a result, they may have the wrong impression or an incomplete picture of your capabilities and strengths.

The women interviewed were consistently top-rated and viewed as "go-to" resources within their companies and/or field. They defined their leadership brand and used their unique strengths to get the job done. Like them, you must know your strengths and build your brand so that you can consistently demonstrate outcomes based on that brand. Information on how to create, market, and protect your leadership brand is available on the book website www.disruptitleader.com/SheDisruptsIT

Should I stay or should I go?

Let's go back to Andrea's story at the beginning of this book. Andrea was battling with this question when she was passed over for another promotion. Your self-confidence really comes into play when you are considering the possibility of leaving your company or making that leap of faith to move to a new position. Not that I am advocating going into the office tomorrow and handing in your resignation — many of you are the breadwinner in your family, and a choice to leave has many implications. But put aside the fear of the unknown, and take a moment to think through your options. You can stay and just accept what is happening to you, you can stay and change what is happening to you, or you can leave and find a new place that fits you. And yes — leaving is risky, but don't make that the reason you don't put that option on the list.

> "I realized that staying in one job and one company for my whole life wasn't going to be the solution, that I had to go where the opportunities were. I took a lot of risks. Some of those worked out, some of them didn't, but it was a learning process." (Anna)

Confidence and courage extend to the management of your career. Sometimes it's the confidence to do the unexpected. Some of the women I interviewed left their companies to start their own businesses or to switch careers completely. For you, it may mean mustering the courage to step outside of your comfort zone to take a role or project in an area that is unknown for you or one that will stretch you beyond your current capabilities.

> "I think that people staying in one role too long is really a mistake, and I think companies allowing people to do that is really the company's mistake." (Alice)

Some panelists experienced this when switching to a company with a different culture or switching functional areas. Adopt a mindset that is willing to take risks in order to get to where you want to be or to go to where the opportunities are. Playing it safe may keep the paychecks coming in, but it will not get you the satisfaction of reaching your definition of success.

"I think people grow when they force themselves into situations. Take those risks. Get out of your comfort zone." (Rebecca)

Drive change and take risks

"Having a can-do attitude is the essence of it for me." (Taylor)

* Are you willing to drive the change? To step up to acknowledge what you bring to the table and to make a difference? That is confident leadership.
* Are you willing to push the limits within I.T. and go beyond the status quo or business as usual? That is confident leadership.
* Are you willing to personally take a risk and change? Do you identify opportunities and step up to make them happen? That is confident leadership.
* Do you constantly look for how things can be improved? That is confident leadership.
* Do you set high expectations for yourself and for your team? And do you follow-through on those expectations to translate a vision into reality? That is confident leadership.

So the question is — do you really want to be a leader? Because leaders take risks. Leadership is not about being the expert in the room — you will need to have the confidence to lead those who are smarter than you. Leadership requires vision and the courage to go after what no one else sees — whether it's the new product, the new way of doing business, the transformation of a team, the delivery of a project, or the stabilization of the operation.

"Go with confidence and be willing to say take the risk, and be willing to do things that are outside your comfort zone." (Rebecca)

In order to support innovation from team members, leaders must be willing to take calculated risks.

> *"Innovation is being able to say… what can we bring to the table that we don't have in the market today? What can we actually leverage in our organization that we can capitalize on?"* *(Erica)*

Every woman I interviewed spoke about the value of having several roles and/or jobs. Some changed companies; others stayed in the same company but changed roles. However, all of these successful women had a history of changing or redefining their roles within 1 to 3 years. They viewed this openness to change as an important contributor to their development and to their ability to gain new perspectives, gain experience, and attract supporters to their network. Changing or redefining roles was also crucial in their exposure to different areas of the business and/or the company. Those women who had the opportunity to be in Chief of Staff or Strategy Development roles or to work in roles that provided exposure to various areas of the business spoke highly of the role such experiences played in their development as a leader — and in the development of their confidence.

Be resilient

What does it mean to be resilient? Successful women are persistent and tough minded. Resilience allows them to focus on the end result and push through the disappointments and opposition along the way. They are used to swimming upstream — to going against the flow of what others expect of them. And they don't give up.

> *"I never took no for an answer, and whenever people shut doors on me, I kept going, knocking on the door until it opened. I think that made a huge difference."* *(Lucy)*

Successful leaders retain their confidence in the face of opposition or in spite of not receiving support from others.

"The key for a woman is to believe in herself because when a woman tries to achieve something that's out of the ordinary, the view the world may have is, 'That's ridiculous. Why are you doing this?' And so if she believes in herself, then she can do it regardless of what others think." (Mia)

Successful women refuse to set limits on themselves or accept the limits placed on them by others. They take a long-term view of success versus being overcome by the interim battles. They also put leadership challenges and other issues in perspective — they do not allow those things to impact them personally. As discussed in the section on the personality traits of these leaders, their self-confident, undaunted perspective on work and life challenges feeds into their success.

"... don't be intimidated if, when you hear other people speak, it sounds like they're so knowledgeable, and that whatever you say will pale in comparison. Recognize that you have your own talents, your own skill set, and exercise that." (Charlotte)

Although they may have concerns about being viewed as aggressive, many of these participants still advise women to be assertive — and to speak up! In the words of Charmaine:

"You speak up. You let people know what you want. You go talk to folks and say, 'This is what I'd like to do.' Find out if they're willing or able to help you with it. Be your own advocate."

Taking risks also means facing rejection and failure. Not every decision you make will be a success. Great leaders learn from their failures and then put the past behind them. This includes being deliberate about rebuilding confidence after a failure, loss, or disappointment.

"You get knocked down again, and you just get up and you keep going, you have to have that resilience." (Lucy)

One key tip from the panel is to "not let it get to you." How? By putting failures, disappointments, and opposition in perspective. As critical as the assignment, job, project, etc. may seem to be,

"Don't take it all so seriously. It's just part of the game of work." (Aaliyah)

Words to live by!

Be FEARLESS

The ability to be fearless will not occur immediately — and the skills are developed over time. For example, going on job interviews is a great way to keep in touch with your value in the marketplace. When was the last time you looked at the positions available within your company or in the marketplace? Is your resume up to date? Do you know the market for your skills? If you are not marketable — what do you need to do to be marketable? How can you update your skills and experience? Get out of your own way. Use the mantras at the end of this chapter to start the reprogramming!

"Be fearless in terms of going after what you want in your career and your goals. Be aboveboard and don't be afraid to make a mistake or be afraid to fail." (Alexis)

Embrace your EGO!

"Males have a great ego and women tend to question their abilities.... [so] have that ego!" (Olivia)

Let's turn that dial from questioning and self-doubt toward having confidence and a female ego! Ego is being strong-minded — even if you are at risk of being called the B* word! While being aggressive may impact your likeability, being nice (likeable) doesn't get you the authority you need as a leader. You need to be your own advocate and not wait on someone else to stand up or speak up for you. It's good to remember that your unique skills, ability, strengths, and accomplishments have resulted in your current success. So set your goals and focus on them — not on how you think you will be perceived. Focus on the outcome.

> *"[W]omen have to stop worrying too much about how they're going to be perceived and focus more on what they want to accomplish." (Chloe)*

Be aware of the personal limits that you may be putting on yourself because you're afraid to go against expectations. For some women, that may mean speaking up (and speaking louder!). Press in and make your voice heard. Forget gender and ethnicity — you are a leader in I.T. — act like it! Don't be afraid to make waves and be different. Don't be afraid to contribute or to ask that provocative question. Or to disagree with the direction of the room. Take confidence from your strengths and value, and step out to do it. Understand that there may be a negative reaction that has nothing to do with your gender or ethnicity — and be confident enough to work through that and face the opposition. Because when you are in that discussion, you are who you want to be — a member of the team who is being challenged based on content, not on the external package!

Be confident in your unique qualities and skill set. Have the courage (and the ego) to bring all aspects of your expertise and personality to the workplace. What are your strengths? What is your brand? What is your value? Make that your daily mantra! Support the expression of your ego every day by leveraging your leadership brand.

Speak up with confidence!

* * *

Consider the following scenario. Jane and Tom presented in a leadership meeting with the manager (let's call him Tony) and peers. At the end of the meeting, Tony pulled each one of them aside and said, "Great presentation! You really nailed it." Here's how each of them responded to this compliment.

Tom: *"Thanks, Tony. I really focused on driving the recommendation through, and I could see that we got the commitment from the team. You know I've also been meeting with our business partners and will present this at their offsite meeting next week. I know I'm ready to present to your leadership team. Can I work with your admin to get on the agenda for next week?"*

Jane: *"Wow, Tony, thanks for letting me know. I was hoping that the recommendation would go well. I know that there were areas that I need to improve, and I am going to work on making some corrections before I present it further. I think it could be of interest to your leadership team — what do you think?"*

* * *

The message is that women tend to self-edit and second guess positive feedback. Men tend to use the opportunity to self-promote. At the end of the day, Tony will leave with a stronger impression of what Tom has accomplished. In contrast, he could interpret Jane's comments (and her self-editing and fault-finding) as a cue to find additional issues with an otherwise great presentation. This is the difference in communicating across the gender. What Jane thinks she is saying is "Thank you — I know that I was not perfect, so here are my areas that I want to improve". What her boss hears is "I don't think I did a great job — I'm not as good as you think I am, and I need help to get better!"

The women I interviewed spoke of the importance of voice modulation for women. We women sometimes frame our recommendations as a question or as if we are asking for permission. Say the following out loud: "We should shut down the system for an hour to make the repairs." Did your voice go up or down at the end of that sentence? Be aware of phrasing your recommendations as a question instead of as a statement. Get rid of the qualifiers such as "What do you think about..." and "It may be just me, but...." Get to the point quickly instead of spending time providing so much information that your listener loses interest before you answer the question or make your point.

Tape yourself or ask someone to give you feedback on your tone in a meeting. For those of you who are soft-spoken, this is the time to understand whether you are not being heard because no one can hear you! These skills can be developed through training and participating in organizations such as Toastmasters®.

"I really work hard to speak louder, to speak up, and to get engaged. So don't just sit there — get engaged!" (Abigail)

Have the courage to speak up at the meeting — to state your ideas and recommendations or to ask those questions. Find ways to be heard, and stop being afraid to say the "wrong thing." After all, is there really a wrong thing to say? Think about what your male counterparts say at meetings. They are willing to say anything — to just throw it out there. Why not you? Are you spending too much time thinking about the perfect question, the smart statement, the factual comment? Are you waiting for the "right moment" to throw out your idea? Are you allowing yourself to feel intimidated by the titles or experience of the others in the room? Then you have probably experienced having the man sitting beside you speak up and have his recommendation applauded while you were waiting for the "right moment"!

Hold fast to your core values but be willing to change

* * *

The personality change — my personal journey: As a person from the Caribbean who was transferred to the US back in 1993, I had to make a cultural shift. That included making changes in the way I spelled (from the British way to the American way) and in the way I spoke. It struck me one day when I participated in a training session that was videotaped. Before then, I thought I was a great presenter. However, when I looked at the tape (yes — it was back in the day of VHS), I saw someone who spoke so softly, you had to strain to hear her voice, who spoke so fast it was difficult to hear the words, and who pronounced things in such a way that the listeners couldn't understand her.

I had a choice. I could stay in my comfort zone (after all — my speaking manner was based on my background and upbringing), or I could change to fit into the new (American) culture I was now a part of. I chose to change. For me, that meant speaking louder and making the effort to speak slower. It started by going to training that helped me learn how I was seen as a presenter, getting (and accepting) feedback, and working on making changes. I took opportunities to practice, practice, practice, and continued to ask for feedback. I learned techniques that helped me to slow down, speak clearly and (yes) to pronounce words the way they are said in the US!

* * *

Successful women determine what they need to accomplish and can tailor their personality and the way that they interact with people in order to achieve their goals. This process begins with understanding and acknowledging your core values. Some spoke about having to make changes in their personal style in order to take on this characteristic. Ava spoke about her transformation when she left corporate America to be an entrepreneur:

"From a business sense, I think I was more introverted and a shyer type when it came to business. But I had to put that aside and just become a very outgoing, aggressive, salesy entrepreneur type, to run a company — my own company."

This does not contradict the earlier commentary on being authentic. In fact, these women spoke about the importance of incorporating change while being true to their core. In all cases they described their transformation as premeditated and deliberate, and occurring in alignment with their core values.

"I think it's best to be true to yourself, and to also know where your ego or other personality patterns may not be supporting you. These aren't necessarily who you really are — it may just be how you operated before." (Savannah)

While your external behavior and the expression of your personality are changeable, your core values should not be. Each person needs to take their own journey to determine where their boundaries are — how far they are willing to go to make changes to themselves without impacting their core values. It could be that you are naturally introverted, but as a leader you will need to adopt behavioral changes that allow you to take on extroverted behaviors.

Some introverts adopt the external behaviors of an extrovert but also realize that, since at their core they are introverts, they need time to recover their energy through time alone. Your personality may be one that does not feel comfortable selling, but as a leader, you need to market/sell ideas, market/sell yourself, market/sell your people. If you determine that the changes required could compromise your core values or your leadership brand, then you need to make a decision. That could be the decision to move to a company, industry, career, or team that is aligned to who you currently are — and does not require you to change in order to be successful.

> "[Y]ou really have to understand your personality and what you are willing to change to fit into that group and decide you're willing to make that sacrifice." (Sarah)

Examine your behavior in your current environment to determine behaviors that may be holding you back — those behaviors that are required to be successful in your current work environment or culture of your company. However, as one or the participants warned,

> "...you can't change yourself so much to a point that it looks fake. You can't do that either, so you have to find that right balance." (Paige)

Take a step back and see yourself as others may view you in the room. A room where everyone else is talking — except you. What impression are you giving? How do you think you are being perceived? If you cannot answer this question for yourself, go to someone you trust and ask them for feedback on your meeting presence. Are you seen as a contributor or as the silent (and therefore invisible) party? Women in I.T. suffer from the (in)visibility syndrome. They are visible because they are different. They stand out as one of the few women in a room full of men — even more if they are women of color. Yet they can be invisible because they are quickly ignored or forgotten if they do not speak up or contribute. Is that the perception you want to leave behind?

"There is a stigma with being a woman who speaks her mind and says what she has to say and won't take any crap. The word bitch *comes to mind." (Chloe)*

As discussed earlier, women experience gender backlash when they act contrary to stereotypic expectations. For example, studies show that women who are assertive experience the negative connotations of not being liked. The same behaviors of assertiveness, forthrightness and directness that are applauded in men as great leadership traits are used against women to criticize their effectiveness. However, women who exhibit behaviors that are nurturing, caring, nice, or likeable are viewed as ineffective leaders. and their authority is questioned! It was interesting to note that all of the successful women who were interviewed recommended adopting assertive behaviors to get the results.

Conclusion — The Confident Leader Toolkit

Now that you know how to be a confident leader, here are some tools that you can incorporate immediately to support your growth in this area.

* <u>In a meeting? Find a way to step up and facilitate.</u> The power of the pen on the whiteboard can put you in control of documenting decisions, asking questions, controlling the ideas in the room, and being the person to drive towards a successful meeting outcome. But watch out: don't offer to take the notes that no one sees (e.g., typing away at your own computer while others speak). This is about leadership, visibility, and contributing — not administrative work!

* <u>Run towards the fire.</u> Is there an opportunity that could yield a tremendous result if it works? Do you have turnaround, transformation, or collaboration skills that can make the difference in that failing team or project? Do you have an idea that could be a game-changer? Sometimes the risk that you need to take is already in front of you. Maybe you just need to open that door.

* <u>Fake it till you make it</u> *"I would say be confident, and if you're not, pretend you are and keep moving." (Nicole)* Where does confidence come from? You!
* <u>Identify assignments that give you exposure to senior leaders.</u> This could be via a volunteer group, affinity group, networking organization, etc. The goal is to get used to being with people at higher levels — not only to learn from them, but to be in a position to work side by side with them and get used to communicating without fear. Many of the women I interviewed spoke about early assignments that gave them this opportunity and the impact the experience had on developing their confidence.
* <u>Put it in perspective.</u> Remember that in the end, being a successful I.T. woman is the game of work, not a life-and-death outcome. Take a moment each day to focus on what brings you personal joy and fulfillment and to develop your life outside of work.
* <u>Develop mantras and repeat them aloud every morning and evening:</u> Reciting mantras is a great way to improve your confidence. Here are a few, but you can develop your own and add them to the list:
  * I always add value.
  * I am unique and I have a lot to contribute to this world.
  * I can accomplish anything — there are no limits!
  * I will overcome every barrier.
  * I am energized by the possibilities in my future.
  * I will succeed.

Chapter 4

✳   ✳   ✳

You're in the Driver's Seat — Own Your Career!

* * *

It was a great opportunity — and one that surprised her. But it was the difference between visibility and lack of it.

A year ago, LaToya was told that "none of the executives knew who she was." As a result, she was not given a coveted position on the leadership team of her new department head. That was her "wake-up call." LaToya worked hard at establishing her network and reaching out to the peers of her new department head. She made a point of speaking up in meetings, asking questions in town halls, and volunteering for additional assignments that broadened her experience and visibility. She also started to explore opportunities outside of I.T. — and leveraged her network to schedule a series of informational interviews in HR.

Her deliberate efforts led to a special assignment that culminated in a presentation to the I.T. Leadership team. The result? Sponsorship, visibility, and a great new assignment!

* * *

"You need to work your career." (Jade)

Who do you think owns your career? Who owns awarding that position at the top that you are striving to achieve? Your boss? His or her boss? Your sponsor, if you have one? The leadership program that you are enrolled in? The answer is none of the above! The only owner of your career is you! You may wonder how that can be — you don't control the opportunities that you need in order for you to progress. You are not in the succession planning meetings where decisions are made on promotion and trajectory. In this chapter, we will take about how to OWN your career, to truly be in the driver's seat for your every move!

Promote Your Leadership Brand!

Have you noticed those digital billboards on the side of the highways? What is consistent about the companies that advertise using this medium? They realize that they have only a few seconds to get our attention, and they want to make those seconds memorable! You don't need the details of the benefits of the product or service — you just need to remember a few key points. In a good advertising campaign, all the collateral, every word and picture associated with the product, is consistently linked to the core brand message.

The same is true for you! What message are you conveying about your leadership brand? How consistent are you in communicating your leadership brand? Are you using all the available opportunities to promote your leadership brand? You need to speak up and take credit for your accomplishments and results. You need to let others know what you have done. For some of you, that comes naturally, but for many others, this may be uncomfortable. Some of those limitations have their roots in our socialization as girls and women; we're socialized to believe that talking about what we have accomplished is unfeminine. A few years ago, there was a campaign to ban the "bossy" word from the vocabulary when describing girls, due to its negative connotation. This is just one demonstration of the socialization that young girls can receive when they try to step up, speak up, or talk about themselves in a positive way.

In contrast, the research shows that in general boys are rewarded for the same behavior that is called bossy in girls. They are encouraged to be the leader of the team, to be the one in charge whom others follow, and to compete for the top position. Boys are encouraged and praised when they talk about their successes and accomplishments. When girls do the same — they are chastised for boasting (or being aggressive, or not being nice, or being offensive). See the difference?

Of course, the above statements are generalizations — there are men who find it difficult to talk about themselves and to tell others what they have accomplished. There are women who are very comfortable with speaking about their accomplishments and stepping up to lead. This section is for those women (and men) who find it difficult to do so, who suffer from a self-limiting belief that speaking about yourself is obnoxious, or who suffer from the imposter syndrome — that is, the internal self-talk that discounts your success and fuels a belief that you don't deserve the success that you have achieved. It is this type of self-talk that can make it difficult to talk about those areas that promote your success!

So, how do you change? You become your own advertising agent and develop a marketing plan for your career.

Create your advertising campaign!

Think of what a typical consumer products company does. It doesn't simply manufacture a product and then hope that customers find it. The company identifies the features and benefits of their product. The company identifies their market — the people they want to buy their product. The company ensures that they know the channels (for example, social media, television advertisements, magazines, etc.) that they want to have the product appear on. The company would also determine the message that they want their potential customers to remember about the product. This is the information that their potential customers will use to remember and be influenced to buy the product.

You are the product! And the most qualified person to develop the advertising campaign about you is you! What are your "features and benefits," or your leadership brand? What is your market — or the people that you need to ensure know about you? Make a list of those people — your peers, your boss, his or her boss, the peers of your boss, your business partners, your team members, others. What are the channels that you can use to get the word out about you? Make a list of those channels, such as presentations, meetings, project reports, 1–1 with your boss, information meetings with business partners, your performance reviews, affinity groups, special teams, short email updates, etc. Be creative in this list — think of any opportunities that you may have to get the word out — you may be surprised by the opportunities that you have and are not taking advantage of. Finally, hone the core message that you want your market (the people on your list) to remember about you. What are the three words that describe the core of who you are and the value you bring? How can you consistently — in every exposure — ensure that at least one of those three messages is conveyed whenever you write, speak, participate, deliver? More information on how to create and market your leadership brand is available on the book website www.disruptitleader.com/SheDisruptsIT

"If you are going to climb that corporate ladder, you have to know the environment and the players in the games that go on there. And if you decide to do that — then put a game plan together and do it. Because it can be done!" (Jennifer)

Develop your career plan!
You also need to be deliberate about the plan that you will use to move your career ahead.

"We get so wrapped up in our job or whatever's going on in our personal life that sometimes I think we just never step back and say, 'Is my career on the right track? Am I doing the right things?'.... On a regular basis you need to take a day off and think about where your career is and what you want to do." (Alice)

Going back to the consumer products company analogy — would this company just launch a product without a plan? If you have participated in strategic planning exercises at your company, then you know that these plans cover several years — not just the current year! Your greatest product is you, and your career plan is critical to the success of that product. Are you really willing to leave that up to chance? Consider these questions:

* Have you spent the time to develop your multi-year Career Plan (your strategic plan)?
* Do you know the specific actions that you will take over the next 1 to 3 years to fulfill that Plan? These should include the timeline for evaluating or planning your next move (approximately 2 years into your current role/assignment).
* Do you have the right connections to fulfill this Career Plan? If not, who do you need to involve, and how will you involve them?
* Do you really know the requirements of the job(s) at that next level?
* Do you have people who are going to sponsor you and be your advocate for the roles you have on your Career Plan?
* Do you have the visibility that you need (see later discussion on Managing Exposure)?
* When special projects and assignments come up, are you one of the candidates that your managers or leadership team considers? If not, why aren't you?
* Does your manager know your career aspirations? Have you engaged him or her in supporting your Plan?
* How does your current role/job/assignment(s) align to your Career Plan? What will you gain from this role that will propel you forward? Based on your answer to this question, do you need to change roles/jobs/assignments to get back on track?
* What specific actions/opportunities/people do you need in order to meet this year's section of your Career Plan?
* Have you aligned your development plan with your Career Plan? How can you take advantage of the resources offered by your company (training, mentoring, etc.) to support your Career Plan?

Go after that promotion!

"[W]omen have this propensity ... of having to prove through hard work, to prove something before they ask for something. Whereas I think men are more apt to just go and ask for it because they know they can do it. But you know what? Women have to just go and ask for it, too. Don't sell yourself short." (Zoe)

When was the last time you stepped up and asked for that big assignment or that raise? When was the last time you applied for that job at the new level? When was the last time you told your boss that you want his or her job? Could it be that the reason you do not have the success you want is because you never asked for it? The best time to go after that promotion, job, project, is *before* you feel ready.

* * *

Frances was elated!

She just got the call with the offer for the VP job. It represented a promotion for her and an opportunity to round out her career in a new business area. But the salary was not what she expected. She knew that she was being well paid as a Senior Director in her current role, but she had expected a higher offer. She had just attended a Women's Caucus meeting on negotiating and knew the facts about the difficulty women have in this realm. In fact, she had accepted her current position without negotiating the offer, only to discover from her network that others were receiving benefits and starting bonuses that were not offered to her.

She had always assumed that the job offer was fixed. Now she was torn. She feared having this VP job offer rescinded if she should start negotiating the salary. But she also wanted to make sure that she was paid what she was worth. She wanted the job — and the title — but was it really worth accepting less than what she was worth?

* * *

What if you were to remove all of those limits you have put on yourself? One way to do this is to invoke the NATTO Principle (Not Attached to the Outcome). You may ask yourself — how is that possible? I care about losing my job or being promoted! What about when (or if) you negotiate for that role or salary or promotion? If you go into a negotiation with fear of the outcome — you settle for less than what you want.

> *"I am not afraid of anything. Regardless of where I go, I'm not threatened by a job. I'm not afraid to speak up because I know how it is out there. I know what it feels like to be without work. I know what it feels like to not have a paycheck coming in. And I know I can survive." (Ava)*

If you go into a negotiation with an understanding of your strengths and value and your BAFO (Best and Final Offer), then you can negotiate freely. Knowing your value helps you to determine your next steps or actions.

> *"[H]ave confidence in yourself. Push yourself to go to that next level, not when you feel you're ready, but right before you feel you're ready, because you'll never truly be ready." (Sophia)*

Without exception, these women spoke about stepping out of their comfort zone. In some cases, it was to take on a new challenge, a new job. In others it was to speak up in a room of senior leaders. Some made bold recommendations for the business or took on a turnaround challenge. Others stepped up to lead an area that others did not want — and won! It was risky — and not always successful. But they also learned from failure and moved on to a better place — both personally and professionally.

Examine your self-talk. Are you your worst supporter? Are you putting the limits on yourself – waiting until you can "prove" with your current role/ assignment that you are ready? Did you take a look at that job description and disqualify yourself before you even applied? Many of you reading this book can point to a time in your life where you took a risk – either personally or professionally. Or where you were "picked" to do something you didn't think you were ready to do. Think back to that time where you took that leap of faith – channel that inner courage and put it to work in your career. Have the confidence to ask for it! Exude confidence in what you do, in what you say and in who you are. Confidence starts from inside.

Invest in the Product!

You must always be ready and eager to learn. In I.T. you cannot depend on your current skills, knowledge, or experience until retirement. It's important to maintain your expertise and to keep on learning — in short, it's important that you invest in YOU! I.T. is a fast-changing field — what you knew well a few years ago will not support your future. Find ways to keep abreast of trends, technology, and the applicability for your environment.

Senior leaders find ways to re-invent their knowledge by staying abreast of relevant technology, studying the future direction of technology, and considering how to harness technology to drive business results. They develop a broad base of both business and technical knowledge and the ability to translate that into communication that provides value to the person that they are interacting with. Your ability to identify opportunities to learn more about the business of your company, the industry, the leadership, the strategy can broaden your perspective and your value.

Look for opportunities to participate in teams that are broader than your specific area — such as collaborating on special projects or working on special events. Find mentors that can help you acquire information and expertise in the business. Reach out to your business partners and conduct informational interviews. Broaden your reading material to include websites, news feeds, business articles, financial reports that keep you up to date. Read up on your company and the industry. Identify opportunities to engage with projects that will give you that broader business perspective.

Don't underestimate taking the same approach to learn about the various areas of I.T. Rotational assignments, different projects, and lateral job moves can also provide you with this knowledge and experience. If you are not able to connect with a project directly, you can use your network to identify ways that you can volunteer to help a project and in return get the additional exposure and experience.

Network, talk with your business partners, read up on your business, follow the business news. Your department and function exist to drive the business ahead — and you need to be a business person who understands how to leverage technology if you desire to go to higher levels. Sometimes this may seem difficult — particularly if your role is more back-office than business-facing. However, I would challenge you to get out and start building your knowledge. Even the most technical role exists to drive the business ahead — it's up to you to identify that connection. If you cannot identify the connection between your role/project and the business objective, then determine whether you are in the right role for your career objective.

The women I interviewed also highlighted the soft skills that contributed to their success as leaders, including

* effective communication,
* conflict management,
* influence,
* negotiating,
* managing complexity,
* managing stress,
* managing upward,
* confidence,
* collaboration, and
* visibility

They spoke about the importance of communicating when you don't have the answer and the ability to reach out to your team or network for answers (or help). To support their development, they maintain a circle of influence that contains people with a broad range of abilities (e.g., technical skills, business skills) and competencies (e.g., soft skills). As lifelong learners, successful women expect team members to possess intellectual curiosity. These women value excellence in expertise and innovation in their team members. I.T. is a field with constant change and growth, and leaders must encourage and support those team members who continue to invest in building their expertise.

"I do value people being able to do that problem solving, and critical thinking."
(Charlotte)

They spoke about how to use emotional intelligence in their workplace. How to you work with people who offend you? With those who have hurt you? With those who have betrayed you? With those that you can't trust? With those who don't support you and in fact seem to be doing everything in their power to prevent you from succeeding? Successful women find ways to work with people they are at odds with — they get smarter, use the soft skills listed above, and find ways to navigate and deliver in spite of these people. In order to do that, successful women focus on their goals, focus on what they want to accomplish, and find ways to continue to operate as professionals. They build relationships that help to address the workplace politics.

Successful women also use their soft skills to run effective meetings. They read the room, get people to participate, and use their skills to help work through conflicts, differences in communication styles, and personality. Successful women know how leverage the diversity of their members to deliver a better outcome.

"I tell my team, 'You have a lot of value, a lot of uniqueness that you can add to this world; don't let anyone limit you based on your race or your gender."
(Charmaine)

Manage Your Exposure!

Managing your career can be similar to a talent agent managing her biggest stars. She's always looking for opportunities to get their name in front of casting managers. She's always making connections and building her network — because a broad and powerful network increases her opportunities to get her clients the exposure that they need. She has promised her clients that she can get them the fame, success, and exposure that they crave — and she does not want to disappoint! What bigger star do you have to promote than yourself? Many times we find it easier to be that talent agent for our people, our children, or our friends, but we forget the biggest undiscovered talent — ourselves! Take a hard look at your "client list" and reposition yourself to the number 1 spot!

Is your image hurting or helping your career?

"How you dress has an impact on how you're perceived....It's all about presentation.... It's working your brand, its working who you are." (Priscilla)

We discussed earlier the importance of projecting the right image to overcome bias, but the right image is also an important element in taking control of your career. This is a tricky topic for women because it brings up all sorts of questions about physical appearance, dress, hair, and some aspects of our body that in fact we don't control. However, managing your image is not the same as changing your looks. Take a few selfies or ask a friend to take some shots of you for a week as you leave to go to work and as you come home. If you can, supplement those pictures with a few mid-day shots. Then, at the end of the week, take a critical look at those pictures.

Now, for those of you who are already self-critical, this is not an exercise for you to review how pretty, slim or fat, old or young you look! This is about what your image says about you. What would be your first impression of the person in the picture? Write down the words that come to mind. Ask yourself (and if you have friends and family that you can trust with this exercise — ask them) the following questions about the images:

* What role in the company do you think this person has? Is she a manager? Senior leader? Low-level employee? Support staff (janitor/ leaner/cafeteria worker)?
* Do you trust this person? This is a harder question for people who know you to answer! But ask them to be critical — would you trust this person to invest their life savings (just from the image)?
* What magazine cover would you pick this person for? *Fortune*®? *Time*®? *BusinessWeek*®? *O Magazine*®? *Essence*®? *Cosmopolitan*®? *Vogue*®? *People*®?

* What kind of car do you think this person drives? Luxury? Sedan? Sports car? Other?
* What kind of neighborhood do you think this person lives in? Upscale? Middle class? City? Suburbs?
* How does this person dress compared to the others in her company — does her dress style fit within the company's culture, or is it outside of their culture? This is a broader question — and the comparison should be to people at the leadership level you aspire to achieve...not to your peers.

As you review these questions, you may be thinking, "What does this have to do with the work that I am doing? This is all external 'fluff.'" However, data shows that image and perception are fundamental components of executive presence and therefore leadership. People make decisions about you in the first 5 seconds after meeting you. What decision are they making about you?

Think back to an important presentation you attended (or watched) and the clothes of those who were presenting. How did their clothes impact your concentration on their presentation? Were the clothes and accessories a distraction? It's a given that powerful women are evaluated on their dress far more often than powerful men. For example, the comments about Hillary Clinton on her changing hairstyles, her pantsuits, etc., have not been made about men in a similar position. So ensure that you dress in a manner that aligns with the leadership image that you want to project.

What Are Your Career Tradeoffs?

There's a lot of discussion on whether you can "have it all." You can — but you have to be clear on what having it all means for you. For some women, it may be a future that includes some combination of children, committed relationships, and a high-profile career. Others may define success in terms of social commitments, business engagements, and changing career aspirations. The first step is to be clear on what you want and how that aligns with your values and definition of success. The second step? Be prepared to make some tough decision and determine what your trade-offs are. Is it ensuring that you have support and help to take care of your children? Is it having a spouse or partner that is available to be there for the family since you will be traveling? Is it going back to school to get that second degree? Is it developing a new skill or quali- fication? Is it deciding to delay having a family? Is it deciding to postpone promotions and particular types of leadership positions to invest in other personal areas that are more important to you? Is it making a job change or career change?

Do you have a strategy on how you will deal with these questions or situations? If you are going on maternity leave — have you developed your off-boarding and on- boarding strategy? If you are planning to change roles or companies as part of your Career Plan, have you thought about the steps you need to put in place to be ready for that move? If your next step for your career requires an opportunity that is not avail- able in your current company, location, or functional area, have you thought through the process to make that change and the implications for you personally?

One of the key lessons mentioned by the women I interviewed is the fact that they cannot do it all alone. And they cannot feel guilty about asking for help. As one participant put it,

"You can't do it all by yourself. You need help. It's a village. Take advantage of whatever that village is for you, depending on where you are in your life. [For me] it was always about trusting who that person was, and giving myself per- mission to trust." (Taylor)

Conclusion – Are You Ready?

Are you ready to accept the ownership of your career? It takes attitude, commitment, and work, but it is the ultimate investment! Remember that if you are not your own cheerleader, no one else will take on that role for you. Take a moment to look at your calendar and pick the day that you will invest in yourself and develop your DISRUPT IT!® Career Plan — you are worth it!

Chapter 5

✳   ✳   ✳

Play to Win! — The
Importance of Relationships

* * *

*The decision: Andrea had been thinking of leaving her current company for
over a year — actually several times over the past 3 years, if she was honest
with herself. Every time she was about to start the process of calling back a few
recruiters, something happened to keep her hopes up that she would actually
be promoted to VP. First it was the leadership on the big project that (as her
boss at the time told her) would be the final demonstration that she was ready
for that promotion at the end of the year. Then she was told that there was a
freeze on promotions but that she was at the top of the "ready now" promotion
list. That was a year ago, and today three VP promotions were announced.*

*Andrea decided to use her regular meetings with her core team of mentors to
ask them to be brutally honest with her — was she VP material? This is a question that she had asked her boss in their last 1–1. Her boss was careful in his
language — stating that she had all the right potential and had strong support
from his boss and a few of his peers. However, there were "no appropriate positions available," and given the nature of VP promotions, it was impossible for
him to commit to timelines. So Andrea asked the same question of her circle*

of mentors, which included a former peer, two former business partners, a few VPs, and a CIO. Her "board of advisors," as she liked to call them, were people that she trusted to give her an honest perspective — even if she didn't always agree with it! Some were relatively new to her; others had been on her "board" for over 10 years. They were a mix of gender, ethnicity, and backgrounds. Just as important was the fact some did not work in her current company.

Andrea was deliberate about scheduling time to meet with them, meeting with each board of advisors member every 4 to 6 weeks and setting aside time to nurture the relationship by finding ways to provide value to them. In the end, Andrea listened to the advice from her board of advisors and drew strength from their affirmation of her marketability. After she communicated her decision to look for VP positions outside of her current company, her board of advisors supported her decision, expanding her visibility through introductions and connections to key members of their network, helping her prepare for executive interviews, and providing insight throughout the final compensation and benefit negotiation process.

* * *

The story above represents the ideal solution for Andrea, who was introduced at the start of this book. Many of us long to have that "happy ending" — the ideal job, the new business opportunity, the promotion. We have reviewed how to overcome bias, how to find your Superpower and become a Confident Leader, and the importance of owning your career. Throughout this book, you may have noticed a consistent theme — the importance of relationships. Let's take a look at how relationships will help you create your own "happy ending"!

Your Personal Board of Advisors

Successful women build their own personal board of advisors — a personal network or group of resources (their circle of influence) that provides the counterpoint to the male old boys' club. The women in this study found creative ways to develop their own networks, ranging from book clubs, lunch meetings, networks formed around giving back or mentoring others, and other activities. They don't restrict the membership in their network based on ethnicity or functional area. Some of the best networks were those that crossed functional areas. While some women used networks as a form of support (to help navigate through difficult times), others used their networks in the same way traditional old boys' clubs operate — to build connections and relationships, to help each other succeed, to grow their business, to identify talent to sponsor, and to give/receive mentoring.

"...surround yourself with people who believe in you because it's ultimately that type of nurturing environment that makes all the difference." (Mia)

Relationship building also extends to communicating to your network what you want. If you don't, others will assume that you are happy where you are, that you're not looking for a new role or opportunity. Be comfortable about speaking up and letting those in your network know what you have accomplished, what you want, and the help that you need. To do that, you will need to be clear about what you bring to the table (your leadership brand), what your goals are (from your Career Plan), and the resources you need in order to achieve those goals (also documented in your Career Plan).

Keep your network strong. Look for a mix of strengths and styles as you build your network or circle of influence. Pull into your network those people who reflect the qualities that you admire or possess the skills that you need — for example, political astuteness, business or technology savvy, or excellent communication skills. Many women make the mistake of reaching out only when they are in need — during a job loss or other crisis — and by that time, it may be too late. Your network should already be in place. And remember, networking and relationship building is a two-way street. Take the time to know the members of your network, to understand their needs and goals, and look for ways to give back and help others in your network.

Take a hard look at your "board of advisors" and seek diversity in gender, ethnicity, leadership style, experience, and background. Affinity groups and other such networks provide value; however, successful women have a personal network (or board of advisors) that is diverse.

What about Sponsors and Mentors?

While all of the women interviewed spoke about the importance of having sponsors and mentors in their careers, it was interesting that only a few women could report that they had actually received help from sponsors. This however was more of a reflection on the difficulty that women and people of color have in attracting sponsors (compared to their white male peers). The women that had sponsors reported that their sponsors could be active and visible (i.e., known to them), but many times they were unknown and operated behind the scenes, supporting their promotion or rise within the company.

> *"I was at a director level at that time, and I was wondering why I would never progress into being a VP. I could never get past that point. She [my sponsor] was one of the major people that helped make that happen." (Lucy)*

Sponsors were attracted to the potential of these women, gave them stretch opportunities, and also provided the support (the air cover) as they worked on those opportunities.

> *"This person has really been a true advocate for me, and I think because of that I'm going to see things progress within the next several months. This person has really gone to bat for me." (Amber)*

How do you get a sponsor? These women agreed that there has to be an "attraction" — sponsors must know about you, like you, believe in you, and feel confident in you in order to put their reputation on the line for you. As you learned in the previous chapter, it is important to build your exposure, and sponsorship comes as a result of exposure. Ensure others know about your abilities, your results, and your potential. The best advice is to remember that your results are not only a reflection of you — they're also a reflection of your sponsor's ability to select a rising star!

"I had people that believed in me, but most the time they believed in me because I delivered! Sort of interesting. I can't say that somebody just looked over and said, 'Oh, let's do something for her.'" (Anna)

Participants with sponsors had male and female sponsors, but they confirmed that it is still easier for men to be sponsored. Sponsorship is largely based on the ability of the sponsors to relate to their prodigy, and many times it is easier to do that with someone of similar gender and/or ethnicity. However, all these women served as sponsors for other women and were strong supporters of their development and success. They were committed to helping other leaders — as demonstrated in their commitment to mentorship, affinity groups, and leadership development for their teams and companies.

Most of the women that had mentors who were informal and preferred informal mentoring over formal mentoring. They recommended that aspiring leaders seek out others that have the characteristics or skills that they need and ask them to help.

"I've had a lot of accidental mentoring where you meet people who embody things that you value, so you mimic them." (Erica)

A consistent comment was that women need to overcome the fear of asking for help from others — or believing that another leader would not be interested in mentoring them. Many of the women I spoke to had several mentees over the span of their career. They also encouraged aspiring female leaders to embrace an attitude of reaching back and helping those that could benefit from their experience.

"I want to help somebody else get that paycheck. Somebody did that for me. Somebody pulled me up by my bootstraps." (Samantha)

Manage Upward

You must invest the time to build the relationship with the person you report to — even though it may be difficult to do so across gender and ethnic lines. This approach of managing upward is critical to getting support and alignment from this critical relationship.

> *"I think it takes work for us as women to build a personal relationship with people higher than you — your direct managers and others. If people don't know you, it's easy for them to make decisions about you. Those decisions may not always be in your favor." (Jade)*

Managing upward also includes setting clear expectations, communicating those expectations, and managing those expectations.

> *"Communication is super important to me, only because I don't know what I don't know, and I don't read between the lines. Or I should say, I choose not to read between the lines. All I need to understand is, if there is an open communication, what do you need from me, and what do I need from you?" (Nicole)*

The women interviewed recommended several tactics to support this, such as scheduling regular 1–1 meetings with your boss, providing succinct updates via email, and using graphical or one-pager updates. In addition, they stressed the importance of communicating in a style and frequency that is aligned to your boss's needs and communication style.

> *"My style is such that when they get something from me, they know it's not something that I send every day. They pay attention; if I say, 'I need to talk to you,' they know it's something that they need to respond to. I try to make sure that it's relevant communication. It gives them what they need to know at the right moment so that they're not blindsided." (Paige)*

Do I Really Need to Network?

Yes — we are social beings! That means that we depend on relationships and human interaction to determine what we think of each other. Although the corporate culture will influence the way relationships are leveraged, relationships continue to be the foundation of networking and politics. It can be hard for women to see why they need to build relationships for the sake of building relationships. But all the expert panelists agree that relationship building really matters and that it was the reason why they were picked for opportunities. Relationship building can lead to doors opening when you least expect them to. And one opportunity leads to another opportunity and so on. Relationship building is critical, not only for overcoming bias, as we discussed before, but for career success!

Ava provided an interesting way to look at networking and relationship building:

"One day, I went to an affinity group and I learned the true importance of networking. And it was weird because I've heard about networking throughout my career, but it didn't get to me until I heard it put into kickball terms. The presenter said, 'You're a kid and you're playing kickball. Who are the people that you would pick first? Well, you pick all your friends first. And who are the people you pick next? You pick the people who you know can play kick- ball. And who do you pick last? The people you don't know or whose skills you don't know.' He said, 'You want to be picked.' Just that little bit of information has literally changed the way I look at networking."

So how can you be picked? How can you build effective relationships that will further your career? What if you are in a situation where those around you have nothing in common with you? For example, maybe you're surrounded by people who are heavily into sports, and that's just not your interest. Do you ignore the social aspects of the people around you and just be work-focused? The successful women advise that you take the time to learn about the culture you are in and the people you are relating to. Think about it — if you're a salesperson trying to sell a product to a client, wouldn't you spend some time researching that client, knowing who the key decision makers are and influencers are? Wouldn't you try to get some background on their interests? And if that was sports, you would at least try to learn more about their favorite teams and be ready to have some type of conversation with them about it.

Take the time to go to where your organization networks. Do people hang out at sporting events? You don't have to like sports to want to meet and talk with people. Are they on the golf course? You don't have to be a great player to enjoy the interaction. Do they enjoy discussing the score from last nights' game? You don't have to watch the game to get the score and the highlights (that's what the internet is for!). Are you in a culture that where people get together for lunch? What about just meeting someone for lunch in the cafeteria or going out for a quick bite?

Find a way to connect that works for the culture you are a part of. It may mean going outside of your comfort zone…but staying within your comfort zone will not get you the results you want. Networking is about building and maintaining relationships and needs to occur from a place of sincerity. Be committed to spend the time to invest in the relationships in your network — it will take time to build trust. And don't underestimate the power of setting up 1–1 meetings or dropping by someone's office to chat. Networking is not an activity that occurs only after working hours; there are always opportunities to get to know someone during the day!

The Political Game

Are you playing the game of organizational politics but using the wrong rule book? Or have you decided that you don't want to engage in the organizational politics? Whether you like it or not, whether you want to acknowledge it or not, the game of politics is part of every organizational culture. And successful women not only learn the rules, they play the game to win! Here are three common mistakes that women make:

* Believing that hard work is what will get them ahead, while being oblivious of the political game
* Acknowledging that the game exists but making a decision not to play it
* Trying to play the game without understanding the rules

None of those strategies work! Political savviness is about making the right connections and gaining the visibility to propel you to the level you want. Successful women learn the unwritten rules of the game — usually from mentors, sponsors, and co-workers.

So, let's summarize the ways to play the game:

1. **Play for power.** Relationships give access to power — both direct power and deferred power (the power that is provided through air cover and support from a well-connected superior). Relationships provide feedback on your executive presence — that combination of qualities exuded by senior leaders that telegraphs the confidence, charisma, composure, and credibility viewed as promotable. Playing the game may be uncomfortable for you, but you can learn do it in such a way that allows you retain your authenticity. Instead of viewing political savviness as being false or "brown nosing," think about it as being interested in other people, understanding what is important to them, making connections between others, letting others know about who you are, and learning about how your organization works!

2. **Get a guide!** The corporate ladder has been described as a corporate labyrinth for women — since they rarely have the straight upward path that is set up for men. Continuing the analogy, to get through the maze you need guides that you can trust (mentors) and those that can cut through the bushes to provide quicker access (sponsors). The game is different at every company, and mentors can help you learn the rules of your current company and/or functional area. Mentors help you interpret the messages and signals that you will receive and potentially ignore, misinterpret, or respond to incorrectly. Mentors prepare you for the experiences that you will face so that you are not "thrown to the wolves." You need to understand the norms of the company and how to integrate yourself into it. Have you found your guides? If not, have you identified potential guides and developed a plan to build those relationships?

3. **Have a game plan!** You would not try to win a game without a plan. Many companies have a political game that uses the "rules" aligned with a top-down, hierarchal structure. In this game, there are those at the top, and team members constantly jockey for better positions and influence with those at the top. As with game of football, there are standard plays that are used to be successful in winning the game. Our expert panels suggests these political plays provided:

* *Play with the boys.* Collaborate on their turf even if it takes you to the bar, sports game, golf course, or to their lunch group. Take time to learn their game rules through

    i.   Observation: Find out who is successful in the organization and what strategies they may be using to support that success.

    ii. Investigation: Ask questions to uncover the written and unwritten norms of the team or organization. Informational interviews with mentors, peers, business partners, and team members are a great way to determine this.

    iii. Analysis: Based on the information collected, determine what it means for you — and how aligned (or misaligned) you are with the organizational culture and politics.

    iv. Action: Make a decision on what you are willing to do to adapt to the organizational culture and political structure. This includes determining if the environment is one that you want to adapt to:

    "If you get to a company and you start to sense that the culture doesn't work for you, change. It may just be a personal thing, but it could also be being a woman in a culture that doesn't fit for you. You should really change and go find a culture where you fit." (Alice)

    * *Play confidently and aggressively.* Be willing to take risks, and work through uncertainty. Don't wait until you have all the answers to make a recommendation or a decision. Speak up in meetings; speak out and let others know what you are thinking. And sit at the table! Don't take the back row either verbally or physically.
    * *Play visibly.* Be secure in what you know, who you are, and how you got to your current position. Keep your skills sharp so you are always equipped to play. Be consistent to your leadership brand, and treat every encounter as an opportunity to sell your brand. It is critical for you to learn how to market what you

have accomplished. It is as important as delivering results. And it is an absolute requirement to achieve the exposure and visibility necessary to move to senior leadership levels. Your success depends upon it!

"I got this, and I can add value. It's not about me, it's about what I can do."
(Abigail)

4. **Get feedback — and listen to it!** Don't overlook the role of your line manager and peers in the game. You need someone who can provide honest feedback — and you need to be in a position to hear and receive that feedback. Many times just getting the feedback is the challenge — particularly if it crosses gender and/or ethnic lines. You must make your boss, peers, and others comfortable enough to provide the feedback that you need. The women I interviewed state that their best managers, mentors, or peers were those who were honest with them. What they did not say (but implied) is that they were also receptive to that honesty — that is, they were not defensive. In many cases women receive a multitude of feedback that focuses on the positive and avoids the tough conversations that they need to hear. Personally, some of the best feedback I received was from a woman who was brutally honest with me. She was one of the first managers to provide feedback on the aspects of my performance that were holding me back from going to the next level.

Conclusion

In this chapter we reviewed the importance of relationships to a successful career. To successfully play in the political atmosphere in your organization or industry, you need sponsors and mentors. You need a network of supporters to help you navigate the minefields — and to position you for the opportunities. You need relationships so that you can DISRUPT IT!®

Epilogue —
Your DISRUPT IT!® Plan

In this book we have covered the four factors I.T. women have employed in their success:

1. Overcoming bias and building a results-focused reputation
2. Finding and using your Superpowers as a Confident Leader
3. Taking ownership of your career
4. Playing to win the political game though relationship building

So how do you use this information to create your DISRUPT IT!® plan?

Let's summarize the key tools identified in these pages:

1. Assess IT!
    a. Assess your Strengths (your Superpowers)
        To define your leadership brand, start identifying your unique strengths. Once you know your strengths, you can build your leadership brand statement that supports consistent outcomes.
    b. Assess your Personal Network

Assess the strength of your personal support group or network. Do you have the relationships that you need? Who do you need to add to your personal support network? Are you nurturing those relationships? What are your goals for each of the relationships?

c. Assess your Organizational Environment

Find out who is successful in the organization and what strategies they may be using to support that success. Ask questions to uncover the written and unwritten norms of the team or organization. Based on the information collected, determine what that means for you — and how aligned (or misaligned) you are with the organizational culture and politics.

2. Plan IT!

a. Develop your Career Plan

Develop the vision for your career. What is your ultimate goal? Where do you see yourself in 5, 10, 15, 20 years? Create your broad multi-year strategy to support that vision. Then identify the specific actions that you will need to execute in the upcoming year to move your career ahead and align with the multi-year vision. Include the timeline for evaluating or planning your next move (approximately 2 years into the current role/assignment)

b. Develop your Personal and Professional Network Plan

Expand and/or nurture your personal support group or network by developing the tools for each of the relationships (see above) and developing an action plan. Identify and build your personal board of advisors that can support your professional vision and your Career Plan.

3. Execute IT!

Implement your Career Plan and the Personal and Professional Network Plan. Determine the method of measuring and monitoring the results of the plans. Conduct frequent (at least annual) reviews and updates to your multi-year vision and Career Plan.

For more information in developing the detailed DISRUPT IT!® plan, use the tools at the book-supporting website www.disruptitleader.com/SheDisruptsIT

About the Author

Dr. Annette Gibbs-Skervin MBA, PMP, is a Founding Partner of DISRUPTING IT LLC. As an IT Management Consultant, she is focused on global program management, organizational change & process transformation, driving bottom-line improvements in Service Integration & Management (SIAM), Supplier Management, and IT Service Operation Management. She provides her consulting clients with the insights and expertise developed from an impressive leadership background in IT and Procurement. Dr. Gibbs-Skervin has successfully generated millions of dollars in savings, driving operational efficiencies in global organizations. She has a solid reputation for quickly analyzing the current situation, envisioning the future, establishing clear objectives, and rendering successful results. Her collaborative leadership style builds strong high performance work teams by embracing diversity of thought leading to exceptional outcomes.

Her expertise includes outsourcing/ insourcing strategy assessment and design, process re-engineering, operating model assessment/ design, enterprise vendor management, supplier relationship management, contract negotiation, and global program/ project management. Her industry experience spans Life Sciences and Consumer Packaged Goods in Fortune 100 companies.

Prior to starting Disrupting IT LLC, Dr. Gibbs-Skervin was the owner of I.T. Transformation LLC, and held several senior leadership positions at Johnson & Johnson, Procter & Gamble and Information Services Group (ISG), including Principal Consultant, Sr. Director for IT Infrastructure Services, Sr. Director Global Service Center Vendor Management Office, and Director IT Strategic Sourcing. In these companies, she established a reputation as a results-driven business partner, and a transformational leader committed to the development of global talent.

Dr. Gibbs-Skervin holds a Bachelor in Computer Science (University of the West Indies), a MBA in Finance (University of Cincinnati), and a PhD in Applied Management & Decision Sciences (with a research focus on overcoming leadership challenges faced by minority and female IT leaders) at Walden University. She is a Project Management Professional (PMP), ITIL Foundation certified, and has extensive experience and training in Six Sigma Black Belt and LEAN methodologies